Anna Kournikova

THIS IS A CARLTON BOOK

Text and Design copyright ©Carlton Books Limited 2001

The publishers would like to thank the following sources for their kind permission to reproduce the pictures in this book:

Allsport UK Ltd 23/ Steve Babineau 28, Scott Barbour 32, Al Bello 24, 26, Clive Brunskill 1, 6, 14-5, 17, 18, 29, 30, 36, 41bl, 44, 46bl, 47br, Simon Bruty 5, 7, 9, 22t, Phil Cole 19, Darren England 46-7, 47t, 47mr, Stu Foster 12, 31, Robert Laberge 27, M.David Leeds 35r, 37, Alex Livesey 10, 25, 35l, 48, Clive Mason 39, Jamie McDonald 16, Daniel Moloshok 13, Adam Pretty 21, 41br, Gary M. Prior 2-3, 8, 11, 19, 20, 22b, 34, 42-3, Ezra Shaw 33, 38, 40, 45.

Every effort has been made to acknowledge correctly and contact the source and/copyright holder of each picture, and Carlton Books apologises for any unintentional errors or omissions which will be corrected in future editions of this book.

This edition published by Carlton Books Limited 2001
20 Mortimer Street, London W1T 3JW
Printed and bound in Italy

This book is sold subject to the condition that it shall not, by way of trade or otherwise, be lent, resold, hired out or otherwise circulated without the publisher's prior written consent in any form of cover or binding other than that in which it is published and without a similar condition including this condition, being imposed upon the subsequent purchaser.

All rights reserved.

ISBN 1 84222 416 6

Project editor: Luke Friend
Project art direction: Russell Porter
Design: DW Design
Picture research: Debora Fioravanti
Production: Alastair Gourlay

Contents

Chapter 1
The Beginning
4

Chapter 2
Annamania
10

Chapter 3
A Money-making Machine
16

Chapter 4
Anna and Alla
20

Chapter 5
Anna's Guys
24

Chapter 6
The Competitor
30

Chapter 7
The Future
38

Chapter 8
The Real Anna
44

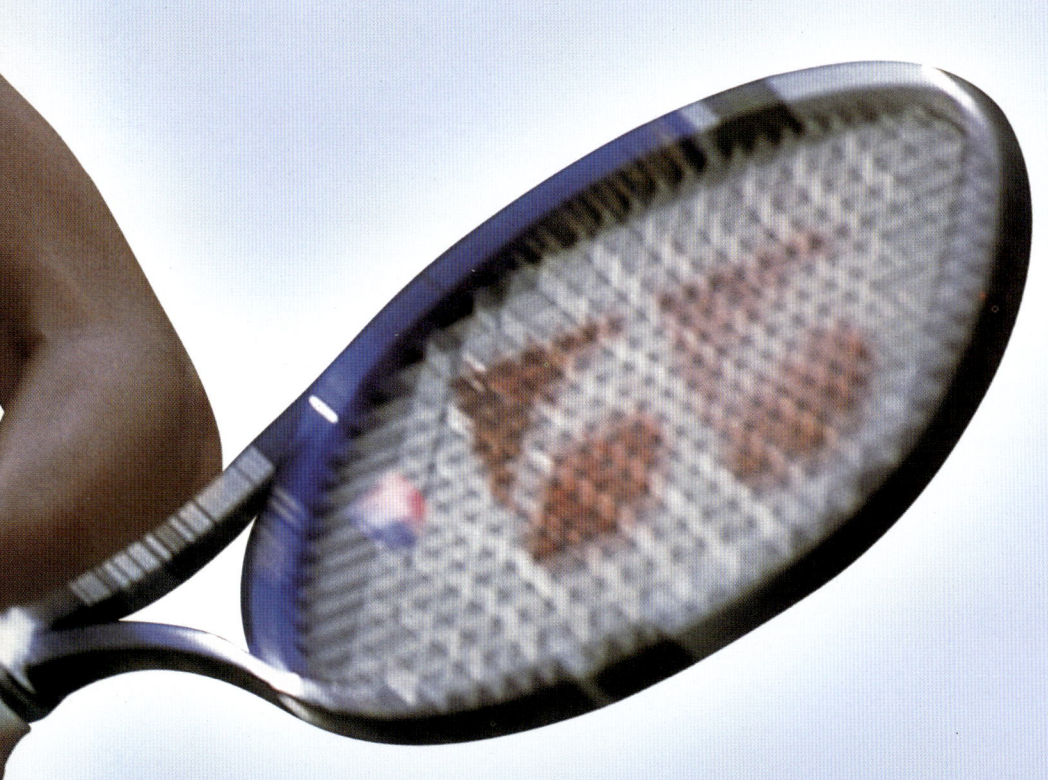

The Beginning

chapter 1

Asked to describe her childhood in Moscow, Anna Kournikova once said, "It was a bit like Cinderella—a tiny two-room apartment, holes in my tennis shoes, and my parents forced to sell the TV to buy me rackets."

If it was a humble beginning, what better way to spawn the fairy tale that has followed?

The daughter of a outstanding amateur tennis player and former 400-meter runner in mother Alla, and a wrestling champion and physical education instructor in father Sergei, Anna began playing tennis at age five, hitting balls in her garden for hour upon hour. Initially encouraged to play by her parents not because they necessarily knew anything about the sport but because they thought it was a healthy pursuit, Anna soon joined a youth club at Moscow's Sokolniki Park, where she played tennis, jogged, hiked, rode rides at the amusement park, gorged on ice cream and started turning heads.

Though her parents sometimes lacked the necessary funds, they saw to it that Anna continued taking tennis lessons and at age seven, she entered her first tournament and enrolled at Spartak, the elite sports academy.

By the age of eight, Alla and Sergei knew they had something special on their hands.

When Anna was nine, she was spotted shagging old tennis balls at a youth club by a representative of Ellesse, the Italian clothing manufacturer, and was also scouted playing the Kremlin Cup by an American tennis magazine publisher. He recommended her to Mark McCormack's prestigious IMG agency and soon, Anna and her mother found themselves relocating to Nick Bollettieri's tennis academy in Bradenton, Florida.

> "I watched a lot of tennis on TV," explains Anna. "I thought I could go there too—to the pro tour. But I didn't think it would happen so fast."

"I watched a lot of tennis on TV," explains Anna. "I thought I could go there too—to the pro tour. But I didn't think it would happen so fast."

Within the year, Anna was traveling to such exotic ports as Paris and Messina, Italy to play tournaments, winning her first Florida junior circuit event as an unseeded player.

The decision to leave Moscow and Anna's father was not easy, said Alla Kournikova, but one she saw as necessary and one she soon began appreciating. "It was something that was difficult for us and there have been some sacrifices," Anna's mother told the *New York Times*, "but believe me, we are not dying here in the U.S. Life is not all that bad compared to back home."

Anna learned English by reading menus. And she would end up spending nine years

in all training under the watchful eye of Bollettieri, who has had seven No. 1-ranked players, but none, it can hardly be argued, with both the tennis talents and the personality of Anna Kournikova.

"I have seen them all, but this one actually frightens me," Bollettieri told the *New York Times* when Anna was 10.

"This little girl walks on the court and there's no two ways about it—she knew who she was and she wanted all the attention," Bollettieri later told *GQ* Magazine. "She was not overly polite. But you sort of overlook that. We got along fine and as she got prettier, she knew how to market it and she found she had a gift for gab."

When you're featured in the *New York Times* at age nine, it's not hard to imagine why you would find the attention both as nothing special and tiresome at the same time. "By the time I was 12," says Anna, "every little girl in Russia was trying to wear her hair like mine and playing tennis."

Andre Agassi was so charmed by Anna that he invited her to dinner. But Bollettieri still did not know quite what to make of her, as she demanded his attention at all times. "She was stingy with her focus, she didn't give a damn about anybody else," Bollettieri told the *Dallas Morning News*.

But, he always had to concede that Anna was quite something special. "She knows it all," Bollettieri said at the time. "And what she doesn't know, she thinks she knows."

"I have seen them all, but this one actually frightens me," Bollettieri told the New York Times when Anna was 10.

In practice, Anna was beating older boys with regularity, including the 2000 men's U.S. Open champion Marat Safin. "She enjoyed beating me because she beat me all the time," Safin told the *Dallas Morning News*. "Everybody was telling me, 'How can you lose to this girl? It's not normal. But I was losing to her the next day.' "

By 13, Anna was beating 16-year-olds at the Wimbledon girls singles tournament, emitting what would become her trademark shrieks as she hit the ball with a force that most grown men could not muster, and shouting "Yes" at every point won.

"I think she can be a great champion one day," said one of her conquests at Wimbledon that year, the much bigger Australian girl, Siobhan Drake-Brockman.

By then, Kournikova was already racking up the endorsements. Her trademark beauty may not have been quite so evident back then, but that was not the case with her tennis skills and particularly her ability to concentrate and to out-think her opponent.

She had also started to develop her infamous temperament, glaring at umpires, questioning line calls and playing to the crowds.

Along with Martina Hingis and Venus Williams, Kournikova was hoped to be just the tonic women's tennis needed as it struggled through the early 90s and an epidemic of injuries to top players, the image problem of domineering parents like Mary Pierce's father, the loss of Kraft, the tour's main sponsor, and, of course, the on-court stabbing of Monica Seles by an obsessive fan.

Kournikova received early attention from her reportedly bratty behavior exhibited at Bollettieri's. Still, Bollettieri was happy to acknowledge her burgeoning talent. "She is too impatient and assertive," he said of the then-12-year-old. "She thinks the world is just going to lay itself before her. But she could be the most unbelievable player. I've never seen anyone with strokes like hers at this age, including Seles."

But by age 13, Anna had already earned a reputation for arrogance, telling reporters who asked about all the attention she was getting, "I've deserved every bit of it. I certainly haven't gotten the attention some of the players we know have. I've watched Venus and Serena Williams play and they're not that good. They've been given more attention than me and they haven't even played tournaments.

"I've put myself on the line. It's not easy to be the No. 1 seed every week with everyone trying to beat you. I've absolutely earned it all."

Kournikova emerged from childhood, if not totally prepared to take on the tennis world, then certainly well equipped to reign over it in some way.

"Of all the stars who have passed through my academy," said Bollettieri, "Anna is the highest profile girl ever in the sport, not only because of her ability to play great tennis but because of her looks and all the other things which put her into a different category.

"She is almost like Michael Jordan in that wherever she walks, whatever she wears, she is different. If an assessment were based on playing ability alone, Anna would have potential. But the excitement and charisma make her someone very special."

And someone very special to watch.

Annamania

chapter 2

You know you're famous when you have a virus named after you. OK, so it was a computer virus. But so well-known and, more important, well-liked is Anna Kournikova that a computer hacker from the Netherlands last February offered e-mail servers what they thought was an electronic photo of Kournikova, obviously knowing that it would be too big a temptation for most to resist.

He was right, of course, as the computer virus slowed down e-mail systems worldwide and even forced some companies to shut down their e-mail entirely. Comparing the virus to last year's "I Love You" virus, which shut down computer systems and cost companies tens of millions of dollars, one computer expert explained, "Last year, everybody wanted to be loved. This year, everyone wants to see a photo of Anna Kournikova."

For the last several years, it has become increasingly clear, everyone wants a part of the phenomenon that has become known as Annamania.

Anna herself can hardly hide from it anymore and gave her thoughts on the matter in an interview last year with *GQ* Magazine. "There are a lot of pretty girls, cute girls, whatever, out there," she said. "If I'd be [ranked] 500, nobody would know. It's that I have a good personality and am a good tennis player—that's what creates this situation."

This "situation" has made Kournikova perhaps the most popular female athlete on the planet and acknowledged as one of the most searched-for athletes on the internet.

Looking for news, gossip, insight or photos, photos, photos, look no further than such websites as MegaKournikova.com, Anna4ever, Amazingly Adorable Anna, Annasworld, Anna Kournikova's Palace, Anna Kournikova rules, All Anna Hotter than Hot. There's even Strictly Anna; a website devoted to links to yet more Kournikova sites.

Several estimates have put the total at more than 20,000 website pages devoted to her in all, and on e-Bay you can buy one of a selection of collectible photographs of Anna.

At every tournament, male spectators in particular, practically fall over one another to catch a glimpse of her while shutters click continuously. Indeed, a survey of all the national newspapers in England during Wimbledon 1999 revealed that on one Tuesday alone, there were 22 photographs of Kournikova. The only player with more that day was Wimbledon contender and native son Tim Henman with 23.

The Evening Standard gave away free Kournikova posters to everyone who bought a paper at the All-England Club, while *The Sun* promised its readers that it was the official Kournikova paper of record and as such, would feature prominent pictures of the tennis star each day of the tournament. Known for its nude pictures on Page 3, the paper ran a provocative photo of Kournikova the week before the tournament started.

Even those who have admitted they would not consider Anna a friend say Kournikova is a positive for women's tennis. Like top player Lindsay Davenport: "She's probably the first player after Gabriela Sabatini to bring sex appeal to the game," Davenport told the *Dallas Morning News* in the summer of '99. "With all the attention she gets, she's bringing people to the game. And she can play tennis. But I'm sure sometimes it's a no-win situation for her."

Kournikova attracts record crowds at nearly every tournament she plays, and she is constantly showered with gifts. At one tournament a couple of years ago, a teenage fan gave her a necklace with his phone number attached to it.

"It's quite amazing to stand on the court with her," said mixed doubles partner Jonas Bjorkman last year, "and see so many guys going nuts."

And Kournikova, with a new, seemingly more provocative outfit for every public event as well as tournament, certainly doesn't seem to mind the attention.

Even her agent agrees. "It is something innate in her. These are things that can't be taught," Phil de Picciotto told the *Washington Post*. "And these qualities of hers are certainly assets because they distinguish her from the stereotypical athlete. She doesn't act in a manipulative way, but she certainly understands that the cameras follow her, and she is comfortable allowing them to do that."

She has been voted one of *People* Magazine's "50 Most Beautiful People;" has appeared in a major motion picture ("Me, Myself and Irene," starring Jim Carrey); and has had so many ballboys bruised by fighting over her discarded sweatbands that there was actually a rule instated for the ballkids at one tournament that they were not to stare at her.

At the tender age of 16, Kournikova told *Sports Illustrated*: "It's human nature for people to notice [me]. If I had plastic surgery to make me look worse, maybe that would help. People ask me, `Why do you have to look good on the court? Why not just play?' But to me, whenever I'm on the court, it's like theatre and I have to express myself. Why should I have to look ugly just because I'm an athlete?"

At the Australian Open earlier this year, Anna was asked if she considered her performance on the court secondary to her appearance. "I wouldn't be here if I wasn't playing tennis, right?" she responded defensively. "So it doesn't matter how I dress. . . Nobody would talk about what I was wearing if I wasn't playing tennis."

Her confidence and overall attitude, however, often comes across as arrogance, for example, her remark to the *Sports Illustrated* reporter after passing a staring fan who offered her a "hello" at a tournament in California—"It's like a menu," said Anna. "They can look, but they can't afford it."—was widely re-printed and often exaggerated.

If this is not one supremely confident young woman, then no one is. But again, Anna Kournikova always manages to be able to pull it off. "There's an aura around her," Claus Martens of Adidas told *Sports Illustrated*. "The way she acts and walks, the whole appearance. And believe me, it was there when she was 11 years old."

Echoed Jim Courier: "She's a born diva. It's amazing how she's able to make it up as she goes along. That's a thing of beauty, too."

At an exhibition match earlier this year in China, Anna showed growing maturity when she explained that she is now simply used to all the attention, that it hardly fazes her anymore and that she tries to take it as a compliment.

"I'm really flattered people are interested in me," she said. "I just want to give back to them, play well. I'm just really excited to have so many good fans. I don't worry about security or crazy people. Sometimes it gets pretty wild, but I know it's like, maybe they have this one opportunity of seeing someone they really like one time a year and I would probably be the same way if I was to see some other famous person. But I'm really just excited that people are into tennis and they like me."

Jim Courier: "She's a born diva. It's amazing how she's able to make it up as she goes along. That's a thing of beauty, too."

A Money-making Machine

chapter 3

If there was ever any doubt of the commercial influence of Anna Kournikova, you need have looked no further than the three-meter billboard on which a bra-clad Anna, hand on one hip, smirked down over London last Wimbledon with the slogan: "Only the Ball Should Bounce."

For the attention the ad campaign received, showing up in virtually every story written or broadcast about Kournikova, the money spent was well worth it. As far as pitchwomen go, Anna has developed into one of the biggies.

Not only is Kournikova the highest off-court money-maker on the professional women's tour, she is acknowledged as one of the top five most sought-after female athlete endorsers in the world and in the same category as the likes of pop sensation Britney Spears.

As with most other matters, Kournikova professes an air of indifference to her earnings potential off the court. "If people are interested, they are interested," she said. "I don't really pay attention."

Like her beginnings on the tennis court, Kournikova is an advertising prodigy with the marketing of the 10-year-old beginning in conjunction with the start of her competitive tennis career, as multi-million dollar deals were negotiated almost immediately with Adidas and Yonex racquets.

It has been estimated that Kournikova earned as much as $15 million in 1999 with the majority gained from endorsements. In fact only $748,000 of that figure came from on-court earnings. All together, such sponsors as Yonex, Adidas and Berlei sports bras have earned her more than $50 million thus far in her relatively short career.

In 2000, Anna was second only to Andre Agassi in endorsement dollars, pitching everything from Omega watches to Pegaso mobile phones. And when she signed a $10 million deal in March with popular Internet search engine Lycos, it made perfect sense, for no other female athlete is searched for as much as Kournikova, who gets twice as many requests as Tiger Woods and Michael Jordan combined, according to the company.

If that's not enough, Kournikova ranked 58th in last year's *Forbe's* magazine's "Worldwide Celebrity Power List," just behind Colin Powell and Donna Karan.

Indeed, Anna's influence is far-reaching. For Adidas, not only does she affect the sales of women's clothing; she sells menswear as well. She is a client of her sports agency's modeling division in addition to sports and has appeared on the covers of

magazines about everything from sports to fashion to finance to travel.

"Who else crosses all the boundaries, the whole spectrum, all over the world," Ulf Dahlstrom, one of Anna's Adidas representatives, told *Sports Illustrated*.

While her competitors often profess resentment for Anna's lion's share of the commercial pie, women's tennis pioneer Billie Jean King said the others should appreciate Kournikova's ability for bringing fans to the game.

"We have a chance to do what no other women's sport has done, to gain equity with comparable men's sports," King told *Sports Illustrated*. "That's done at the box office. It doesn't bother me at all if some of the guys come out to watch women's tennis because they want to see a beautiful woman. Who could hold that against Anna? Still, it is unfortunate when others with a high skill factor don't win the endorsements. Sure, the good-looking guys get more endorsements, but the difference in men's sports is that the ugly ones get their share too."

Kournikova ranked 58th in last year's *Forbe's* magazine's "Worldwide Celebrity Power List," just behind Colin Powell and Donna Karan.

Anna and Alla

chapter 4

When Anna Kournikova left Moscow for Florida at the age of 10, it was Alla Kournikova who took care of everything, including her daughter, as they ventured into the great unknown of professional tennis.

Under those circumstances, it is not surprising that the two are still so close, often dressing alike in matching Adidas warm-ups and finishing each other's sentences. Even though Anna is hardly a little girl anymore, it is clear that Alla is still her best friend and values her mother's influence.

"I could not be out there alone," says Anna.

In turn, Alla is obviously her daughter's biggest fan. "She's a smart little girl and a disciplined girl who follows a straight line," Alla once said of Anna. "She sees what she wants and goes out and gets it. And in every match she plays, she thinks she is going to be the winner."

Alla's enthusiasm for her daughter's career, however, has often gotten her into trouble. Or at least drawn the wrath of others.

Often, Alla Kournikova has been accused of interfering with her daughter's training, causing much aggravation to the coaches at Nick Bollettieri's tennis academy in the early years of Anna's career.

"I've been in tennis 35 years and have never seen anything like Anna's talent," Bollettieri told the *Daily Telegraph* when Anna was 12 years old. "But I'm very concerned that her mother may be crossing that fine line between being supportive and getting too involved."

So intrusive was Alla at Bollettieri's, that they actually had to invoke what they called "The Kournikova Rule," which restricted parents from coming on the practice courts while their children were being coached.

One magazine writer once wrote, "If Anna is a princess, Alla is a queen."

"Mama is the head coach and always will be," Bollettieri told *Sports Illustrated*. "You can't fight mama because she and Anna are very close."

There have been many cases of interfering parents in women's tennis. Mary Pierce actually had to get a restraining order against her father. Jennifer Capriati was estranged for a time from her father.

"Jimmy Connors' relationship with his mother Gloria was positive and Chris Evert's dad Jimmy did a great job too," Bollettieri said. "But I'm amazed how many parents progress very quickly from being a housewife or a lawyer to suddenly becoming a tennis

coach. Parental involvement can be more negative than positive. Sooner or later, the student has to make a stand and the parents have to accept this."

Bollettieri says he has tried to mediate arguments between Alla and Anna. "I would say nice things to Anna if mom was a little bit rough," he said.

But it hasn't been all that easy on Alla either, having all the worries of a normal mother along with the additional concerns of a burgeoning career and the worldwide fame of Anna.

Kournikova's former coach Pavel Slozil says that tennis moms have to be "a little crazy. But [Alla] is positive crazy, not like Mary Pierce's father," said Slozil, who was fired by Anna after 15 months at the urging of her mother. "It's not easy being in her position. She and Anna are like sister to sister, but sometimes Alla must be the mother and sometimes, the father too."

Anna's father Sergei, (above left), a former wrestler and professor at the University of Physical Culture and Sport, stayed behind in Moscow when Alla and Anna moved to Florida in 1992. Sergei travels to tournaments about five or six times a year. "It's hard," Alla told *Sports Illustrated*, "but I'm not one of those people who cries about it. She's my child and I want to be there for her. What else would I be doing?"

Now that Anna is grown up, Alla does not try to tell her little girl what to do quite as much. "Anna still listens to me," she told *Sports Illustrated* last year, "but now she also wants to try everything for herself."

Either way, Anna isn't complaining.

"My relationship with my mother and father is very strong," Anna says. "All parents have to make sacrifices for their children. That is what you have children for. But I think mine are happy now."

> "My relationship with my mother and father is very strong," Anna says. "All parents have to make sacrifices for their children. That is what you have children for. But I think mine are happy now."

Anna's Guys

chapter 5

If you counted every guy who wanted Anna Kournikova to be his girlfriend, including the men players on tour as well as ballboys, fans and assorted website users, the total might number in the millions. If you restrict it to the men who Anna has actually returned interest; it is reduced to a much more reasonable figure.

Anna's boyfriends, or more accurately, speculation about Anna's boyfriends, are arguably documented as much as her tennis career. And on many occasions, most of the questions she is asked at her post-match press conferences have more to do with that topic than her opponent's serve or Anna's backhand.

When asked what she looks for in a man, Anna says, "He has to be sensitive, kind, generous and big-hearted. Looks don't matter."

But, of course, everyone wants specifics. Anna's romantic interests have seemed to shift mostly between hockey stars Sergei Fedorov and Pavel Bure. But there have been other suitors as well, and lots of confusion about who ranks where in Anna's heart.

At one point in the spring of 2000, for example, she appeared to be engaged to both Fedorov and Bure. She was also spotted kissing men's tour pro Mark Phillippoussis in a Melbourne car park and was whisked away from a WTA awards ceremony in a silver Porsche by tennis player, Ecuadorian Nicolas Lapentti.

At the 1999 Wimbledon championship, Fedorov, with whom she has recently reconciled, was the focus of attention as the Russian native and the Russian beauty were often found together, whether at her practice sessions, where he scooped up loose tennis balls, watching her matches, carrying her tennis equipment or strolling in London.

Yet, Anna seemed to enjoy then as she still does, keeping the media guessing about her love life. During that '99 Wimbledon, for example, Anna said she did not have a boyfriend, despite the three-carat diamond ring on her left hand which produced this exchange at one of her post-match press conferences.

Reporter: "Anna, can I ask whether you have a boyfriend?"
Anna (with a smile): " No comment."
Reporter: "Do you have a ring on your third finger?"
Anna: "I have no comment to that. I'm wearing everything all the time, every time different. So it's not like I'm wearing something that means something."

Reporter: "Was it just a piece of costume jewelry, your ring? Because there was a lot of talk about the ring you were wearing."
Anna: "No comment."
Reporter: "Are you engaged to anybody?"
Anna (giggling): "No comment. I can say it one more time, no comment."
Reporter: "But you said you didn't have a boyfriend last time and then suddenly you're seeing Sergei and the ring and stuff. Everybody draws the opposite conclusion, they're confused. They want it cleared up."
Anna: "No comment, sorry."

"She enjoys the game of it," her coach, Eric Van Harpen, told *Sports Illustrated*. "The secrets. She enjoys just saying `perhaps.' What woman does not want to say `perhaps'?"

Anna had been linked romantically to Fedorov, the 31-year-old Detroit Red Wings forward, since she was 15. But she even keeps him guessing. Once asked by a hockey fan if Sergei was her boyfriend, Anna hissed "He wishes."

At one point, she actually tried to explain that it was a case of multi-cultural confusion that made so many question her true intentions. "In Russia, there is no word for boyfriend," she told *Sports Illustrated*. "You're either married or you're friends. Maybe people want to see Sergei as my boyfriend, but he's just a good friend of mine—a very good friend. Our families are close. We came from the same background and we have a lot in common."

Anna's mother Alla has appeared to approve, saying "They're friends, it's normal" of Anna and Sergei.

Still, questions persist about their age difference, though not as hounding before Anna was of legal age. To Anna, it is a sore subject. "It doesn't matter how old you are," she says. "Why should other people tell me who I should be friends with or what I should do? They're not perfect themselves and it's none of their business. Some things are personal. You wouldn't say what you did with your wife, either."

When Anna played in the '97 U.S. Open at age 16, Ferdorov attended Anna's matches. The *New York Post* wrote a story on their age difference, quoting a member of the District Attorney's Office as saying Fedorov better watch his step with a minor.

Again, Anna was annoyed. "I'll do whatever I want," she said. "At this year's Open, I'll have five boyfriends."

Anna and Alla have lived in Fedorov's $1.6 million apartment in Miami's South Beach, the same complex where Bure (above) moved into an apartment a few floors down. Reports that Bure gave Anna a $650,000 engagement ring sent Sergei into a funk and prompted him to give Anna a bouquet of more than 200 roses, though the romance with Bure ended, according to reports, within five weeks.

As late as March of 2001, when asked who was her current boyfriend, Anna, wearing a bracelet with Sergei's name on it, replied, "I don't have any new ones. I only have my old one. But I don't think I'm going to make it more difficult for all of us by saying who it is."

Under any circumstances, it cannot be easy being Anna's boyfriend, which she admitted in *Esquire* magazine. "Boyfriends have to understand me and my needs," she said. "They need to know what I want out of my life and about my strict regimen."

"If you have a good understanding," she told the *Times* of London, "it all works out. It is not true that you cannot have a private relationship in the public eye, but it does depend on the person you are with."

Anna's boyfriend must have patience not just with the temperament of Anna but also of her sometimes overly protective mother. The Russian newspaper *Komsomolskaya Pravda* blamed Alla for breaking up the relationship between Anna and Pavel Bure.

But somehow you have to believe that what Anna wants, Anna usually gets.

The Competitor

chapter 6

At 16, anything seemed possible. In 1997, Anna Kournikova became only the second woman in the Open era to reach the semifinals in her debut at Wimbledon, joining Chris Everet, who accomplished the feat in 1972, and there seemed to be no doubt that before long, Anna would be holding the famed silver plate aloft.

Now, however, she is often compared to Gabriela Sabatini, who won just one Grand Slam title despite expectations of greatness, and was ultimately remembered more for her beauty than her tennis.

Kournikova, ranked eighth in the world at the end of 2000 and injured for three months of 2001 with a stress fracture of her left foot, has reached the fourth round at a Grand Slam tournament seven times, each time losing to a seeded player.

At the 1998 Ericsson Open in Miami, she beat four top-10 players four days in a row, the first time in 11 years that had happened, to reach the final.

She has reached tournament finals in Key Biscayne and Hilton Head. At the WTA Championships in New York in 2000, she lost to Martina Hingis, the world's No. 1-ranked player, in a close semifinal match. And in the 2001 Australian Open, Kournikova reached the quarterfinals before losing to Lindsay Davenport.

But she has never won a professional singles title.

"If she won just one major title, she would become the most famous female athlete of all time," says former tennis great Charlie Pasarell.

But Anna's former coach Eric Van Harpen, whom she split with in August of 2000, admits it is hard to motivate her. "[What would I say], 'You will have a Porsche?' She has one. 'You will have jewelry?' No."

So he tells her that anyone can be beautiful, but few can be beautiful and a tennis champion. "She loves the applause, she is the queen," says Van Harpen. "So she thinks she must play like a queen. Sometimes though, it is better to play like a beggar."

Anna's mother Alla, however, lauds her daughter's killer instinct on the court and says her fans appreciate it. "It is not just her looks," says Alla. "They like Anna for her tennis."

Indeed, Kournikova has appeared to have a hunger for winning since she first picked up a racket.

"It is not just her looks," says Alla. "They like Anna for her tennis."

She made her pro debut at 14, winning a Federation Cup match for Russia, defeated Steffi Graf in a one-set exhibition in Moscow at 15 and rose to No. 1 in the world junior rankings.

Anna, however, had an opponent even she could not get past.

"I want to turn pro really soon," Anna was quoted as saying at the tender age of 10. "The sooner the better." The powers-that-be in women's tennis, however, would throw up a major obstacle by way of their new age limitation requirements. Jennifer Capriati had turned professional at 13, and Anna was poised to do the same when a new eligibility rule was enacted, limiting the number of tournaments a player could enter (16) before her 18th birthday.

By then, Anna had beaten all of her older opponents in the juniors, winning the Orange Bowl 18-and-under title, the Italian Junior Open and the European Championships while reaching the semifinals at Junior Wimbledon and the quarters at the French Open Juniors.

Anna and her handlers still blame the age eligibility rule for slowing her development as a player and say it put her at a distinct disadvantage compared to Hingis, for example, who was grandfathered in under the old rule.

> "I want to turn pro really soon," Anna was quoted as saying at the tender age of 10. "The sooner the better."

"She was the first player to grow up under the full force of the WTA age limitations," Anna's agent, Phil De Picciotto, told the *Dallas Morning News*. "She was the No. 1 junior in the world, but she was limited in what she could do as a pro. That allowed for a lot of speculative off-court stories."

On court, few have denied her talent.

Anna is a classic serve-and-volleyer, producing both the grace and cat-quick instincts necessary for her to be a great champion. "Anna is a shotmaker," Bollettieri told *Sports Illustrated*. "She has the ability to create situations on the court that very few people can create. And at the net, she's brilliant. She hits volleys from all angles. The only person I could compare her to is John McEnroe."

She also is a wonderful athlete; agile, able to chase down any shot and a powerful serve returner, though inconsistent on her own serve and prone to injury.

Still, she has worked hard to improve and showed that between the '99 Australian Open, when she had 31 double-faults in a second-round victory, and Wimbledon of the same year, when she had just five total in three matches.

"Some people felt she thought it was more important to look good," Pam Shriver told the *Dallas Morning News*. "But you don't fight to get over the yips if you're just about looking good on the court. A lot of people would have fallen away. That showed me something about her character."

Anna won the 1999 Australian Open doubles title with Hingis and appears ever so

close to breaking through for her first title in singles.

Anna has, however, had her problems with her competitors on tour, and not just on the court. Jealousy abounds in professional tennis and Anna feels it is pure envy that has sabotaged many of the relationships she has had with her fellow players.

In Nathalie Tauziat's book *The Underside of Women's Tennis*, she wrote of Kournikova, "I like her, but who does she think she is when she parades around like a queen at the French Open, so absorbed that she does not even notice hands holding out autograph books?"

Tauziat also calls Kournikova in her book "a blonde cash machine," writing, "All the women play harder against her to make her realize that, on court, being the prettiest is useless. If she gets results as impressive as her beauty, she will be the most adored player in history. But if she fails, the system will crush her."

Tauziat later elaborated to the *Washington Post*: "I just don't like the whole system of people talking only about her because she's sexy," she said. "There are other girls who are as good players and better players and they don't talk as much about them."

Other players are even more outspoken in their dislike for Kournikova. Austrian Sylvia Plischke told of several players congratulating her for knocking Kournikova out of the French Open.

And Swiss player Patty Schnyder admits, "I just don't like her. And everybody looks happy when she loses." To which Anna responds, "I think I've beaten her five times in a

row and she's never beaten me, so I guess she's not really happy about me."

Davenport chides Anna for being aloof, saying "hi," one day and walking right past the next, while Hingis, before becoming Anna's doubles partner, needled Kournikova for never living up to the rivalry predicted for the two.

"She's very pretty," Hingis, who is 5-0 versus Kournikova, told *Sports Illustrated*, "but I'm sure she would like to change places with me if she could and have four Grand Slam titles."

Anna does have some supporters, including Monica Seles. "Anna has things the rest of us don't have so yes, some of the players are envious," she said. "But others who know her, like her. Remember, Anna comes from a hard place, so perhaps she should get more credit than some want to give her."

Hall of Famer Martina Navratilova, like Billie Jean King, lauds Anna for bringing fans to the game and said those players who are jealous of her need to "get over it."

"What is she supposed to do, give the money away?" Navratilova told the *Washington Post* of Kournikova's vast endorsement earnings. "Say, 'No, I don't want it. Please don't pay me?' Life is tough. I never got the breaks that I should have gotten. She's good for the game. She brings attention. I just wish she'd play better. She's a better player than she's shown."

That is really at the heart of all the envy and criticism, for Kournikova, for all her talent and all of her appeal off the court, has not reached her potential as a tennis player.

Anna dismisses this. "Forget what the players say, ask the fans," she says. "I think it's normal for people to be jealous. But I've never been jealous of anybody. I've never said, 'I wish I was her.' Honestly, I wish I was me."

Anna's opponents have had reason to resent her fans as well. In one straight-set victory over Capriati in a pre-Australian Open tournament in early 2001, Capriati lost her composure and the match after leading a set and 5-3 in the second, later lashing out at Kournikova enthusiasts.

"It's very distracting and difficult for anyone to concentrate because of all the hype involved with her," Capriati said. "I can understand when people are acting that way for a reason, but when you see people shouting for her in an exhibition match, it's like 'Why are they?' But I think we all know why."

Early this year, the doubles partnership between Kournikova and Hingis, which produced eight titles, ended under somewhat mysterious circumstances, with some reports having the two arguing bitterly, Hingis resentful of the attention showered on Kournikova and Anna eventually breaking down in tears.

Later, Anna said she was crying for another reason, though she would not say why, and downplayed the break-up with Hingis. "A lot of players change partners all the time, so it's absolutely normal," said Anna. "I want to concentrate more on my singles. I'm not going to play as much doubles as I used to. That's it."

Anna's fans can only hope that new focus on her singles play will soon yield her first professional title.

The Future

chapter 7

The biggest knock on Anna Kournikova and to Anna, the biggest insult, is to suggest that somehow she does not care about becoming a tennis champion, that she is satisfied being a celebrity of global proportions and a young woman already rich beyond her wildest imagination.

But talk to Anna about her tennis and she will tell you she is more passionate about her sport than anything, and that fame and financial reward is secondary.

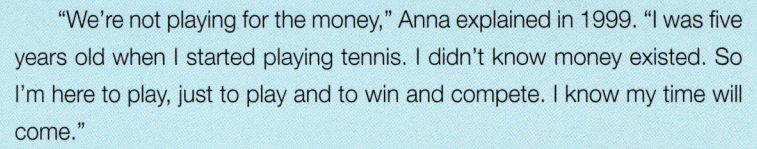

"We're not playing for the money," Anna explained in 1999. "I was five years old when I started playing tennis. I didn't know money existed. So I'm here to play, just to play and to win and compete. I know my time will come."

But when? And how? There is no question her celebrity is here to stay, but what about her prospects for a first singles title and beyond that, a ranking among the top few players in the world, an achievement she has been destined to accomplish since she first picked up a racquet?

The key seems to lie with Anna herself, and her own motivation.

"The question with Anna," Billie Jean King told *Sports Illustrated*, "is 'How badly does she want it?' Does she want to make the most money, like Sabatini did, or does she want to be number one?"

"Anna can become a superstar of unbelievable magnitude," said former No. 1 Charlie Pasarell. "You can tell she's special just by looking at her. She walks like a champion."

And talks like a champion for that matter.

Kournikova bristles when it is suggested that she is more concerned with style and endorsements than her tennis game. "That is completely untrue," she told the *Times* of London. "I am 100 percent focused on my tennis."

Still, Anna is defenseless when it comes to the very real fact that she has yet to win a professional tour singles title. "I can't complain because it's true," she said in January of 2001, just before an injury would force her from the tour. "But I know that I'm playing hard, the ranking is important to me. [No. 8] is my highest ranking so far. I know I'm a good player. I've beaten five number ones in the past five years, so that's a good record and I've beaten almost everybody in the top 20 and in the top 10.

"I feel like this past year was great for me, very consistent and the best year so far."

> "You can tell she's special just by looking at her. She walks like a champion."

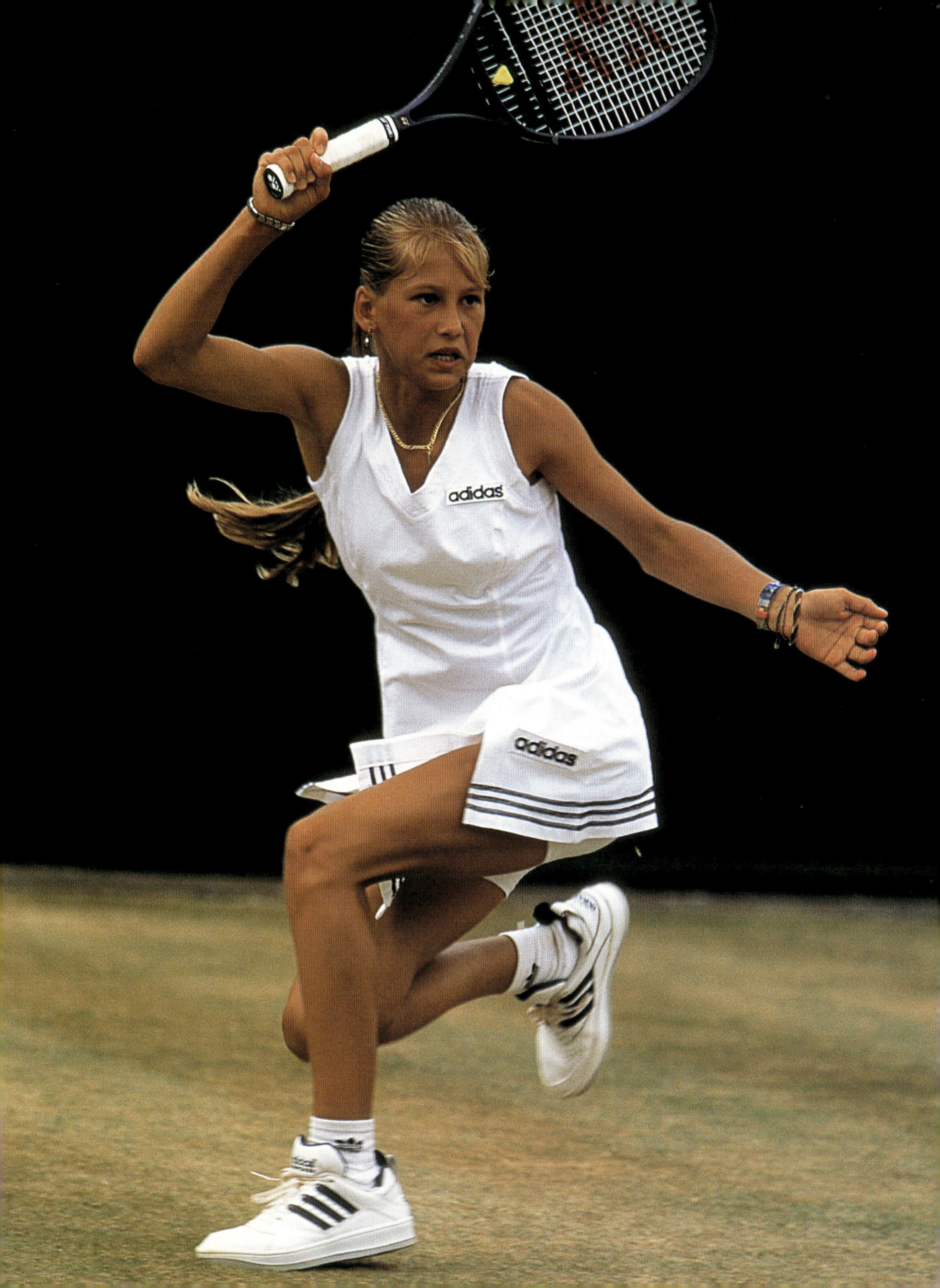
adidas
adidas

Kournikova has had several coaches throughout her career, but is now working under the guidance of her parents after splitting from her last coach, Eric Van Harpen in August of 2000 in part because he told her she was allowing the trappings of fame to distract her.

"My parents are helping me," she said in January of 2001. "And I like it the way it is. My dad [Sergei] is a professor. He coaches. He's a professor at the University of Physical Culture in Moscow. He knows a lot about it. He has a Ph.D in it.

"I'm perfectly fine just like I am. I think I'm playing even better since August. I think that's when my improvement started, when I was ranked 14th."

And what does she think she needs to do to make the jump to a top ranking and her first singles title?

"I just want to continue the way I'm playing and the way I played at the end of [2000] and continue to be consistent in the top eight," Anna said in Sydney in January 2001. "Hopefully this year I can make the top five. That would be what I would like to happen by the end of this year. And in order to get higher ranked, I guess I just have to play much more consistent and just win the big matches.

"I'm getting to the semis of every second tournament I play, which is good. I'm just really excited to go out there and give my best and if I win, it's great and if I lose, I'll keep working. Obviously, the ultimate goal is to win when you're on the court, so that's what I'm trying to do."

Injuries have definitely been a problem and in February of 2001, a stress fracture in her left foot forced her to the sideline, where she has missed events in Key Biscayne, Florida, Charleston, North Carolina, Acapulco, Mexico, Indian Wells, California, and Amelia Island, Florida. In her absence, her ranking dropped from a career-high of No. 8 to No. 12.

"The most important thing for me is to maintain my world ranking," says Anna. "I've improved and I've been playing more consistently. I'd like to improve more and I know that I have to work very hard to do that."

In the meantime, she will continue to endure accusations that she simply doesn't care enough about her tennis.

Often compared with Gabriela Sabatini, the Brazilian beauty who won just one grand slam tournament in her career despite appearing destined for superstardom, Anna's former coach Pavel Slozil said that would be a horrible waste of her talent.

"That would be too bad is she became the next Sabatini," he said. "Sabatini was satisfied with being in the top five and winning one Grand Slam. Anna is capable of more than that."

Anna says she is far too young for people to give up on her. "I think most people forget that I'm 19 years old," Anna said in February 2001. "Jennifer Capriati won her first Grand Slam when she was 24, so I think I have another five years to work on it.

"I'm not saying that tomorrow I'm going to be No. 1 or tomorrow, I'm going to be this or that. I'm just going to keep working hard and whenever it happens, it happens. I know that I'm working hard and that's it.

"You never know what's going to happen tomorrow. Maybe it's the end of the world."

"Like I always say, you can never predict anything," says Anna. "You can never say it's going to happen tomorrow, in one year or five years. I just have to keep working hard. I know that I'm a good player. If I will continue to work, continue to improve the way I've been improving, eventually my game will come together and everything will be fine."

"I'd like to improve more and I know that I have to work very hard to do that" says Anna

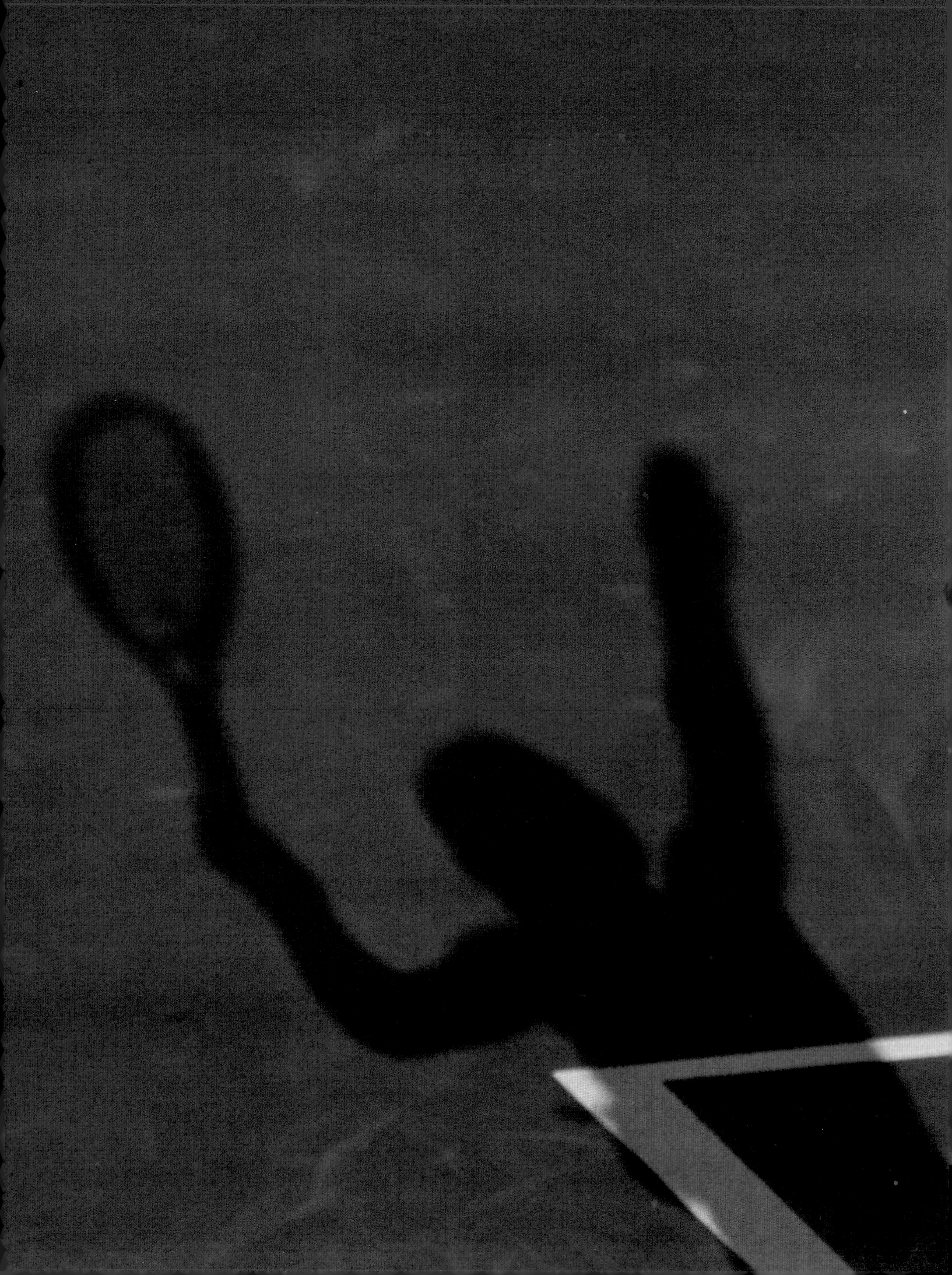

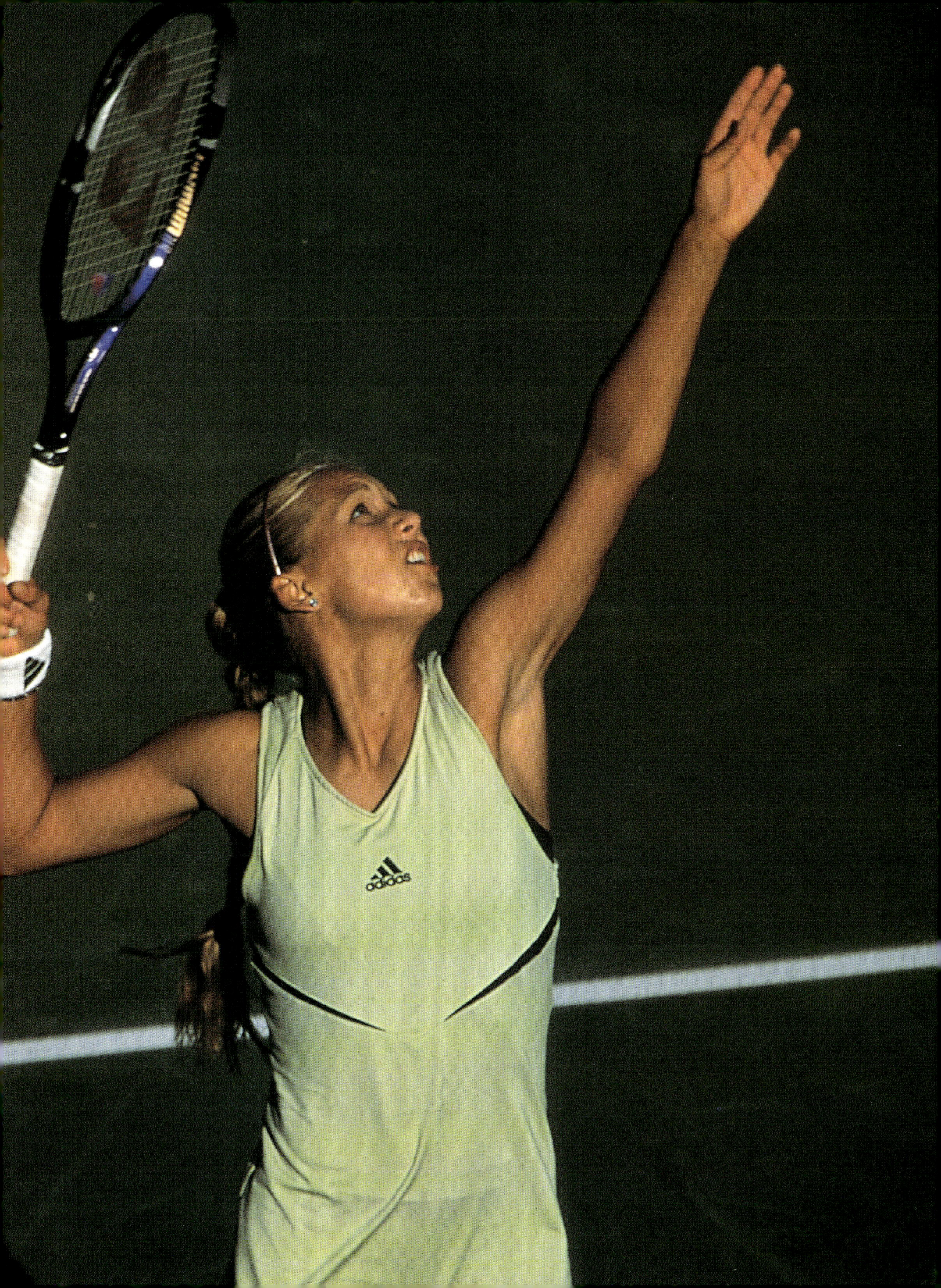
adidas

The Real Anna

chapter 8

So who is the real Anna Kournikova? Temperamental diva? Misunderstood beauty? Overrated athlete? All of the above? Anna would no doubt balk at all the stereotypes about her, opting instead perhaps to have people see her the way she sees herself. Or the way those closest to her view the young woman who's still, at times, a little girl.

"I'm the perfect age right now," she told *Sports Illustrated* just before turning 19. "I can be a little girl or I can be grown up. I can be whichever I want."

Would you feel like you knew her any better if you knew that she collects dolls, loves animals and that her favorite TV shows are *Jay Leno*, *Melrose Place* and *Friends*? How about if she told you she loves listening to music and dancing, and that her favorite bands are Bush and Korn? Or that she likes art, the color black, sushi, steak, Italian food and chocolate?

When she was 13 and already almost famous, Anna still played at painting faces and dressing up.

Less than three years ago, her fame peaking, Anna was quoting lines from movies like *Clueless and* seemingly genuinely excited about her growing celebrity.

Those who suspect her sincerity should know how she feels about such things as religion and world peace. "I like to go to church," she said. "It's so nice and peaceful inside. You come out and you feel clean. Everything dirty is gone."

Her only concern, she once said, is war. "There is enough room for everyone in the world," she said. "Why can't they talk—not with tanks and guns?"

She said she appears to love the cameras because she has no other choice if she doesn't want the attention to distract her completely. "I just try to go out there and play," Anna says. "If I would be bothered by it, that would not be good for me. I have to be cool about it and just not think about it."

The truth is, however, Anna is not always easy to get along with. "She does not suffer fools gladly—or nice people either, for that matter," says tennis commentator Mary Carillo. "She's very self-possessed. She's her own law and she calls her own shots. She doesn't care what people think. Everybody's there to serve her, everybody's her underling."

And yet at times, though most may see her as conceited, she has let down her guard

to expose someone who is insecure just like everyone else.

"There are thousands of beautiful women," she told *Sports Illustrated*, "but how many have the ability to play tennis, to be a personality? If I would be ranked 500, no one would look at me."

Those who are envious of her physical attractiveness should listen to Billie Jean King, who points out the pitfalls that could confront Anna as over the next few years as a tennis player.

"Being a beautiful woman is a lot like being a tennis player," she said. "You know the best of it has to end when you're still young. To be both, as Anna is, can be hard. After all, from age 10, she has heard two things over and over—how beautiful she is and how great a player she is."

Even if you have erected the walls around you yourself, it can still be lonely at times.

"Sometimes Anna must be lost," says former coach Nick Bollettieri. "She never had a childhood. She must wonder what it's like to live a normal life."

But Anna won't accept pity any easier than she will accept criticism. "Normal, what is normal?" she snapped. "That kind of life everybody talks about as normal wouldn't be normal for me. From age five, when I first played tennis, that's all I wanted. From the first, I was so happy on the tennis court. I can't think of anything better.

> "People say I missed out on childhood, but I don't think so. I have had the greatest times playing tennis, winning matches, doing everything I love.

"People say I missed out on childhood, but I don't think so. I have had the greatest times playing tennis, winning matches, doing everything I love. I am a very energetic person. I have never been able to sit still. So it is good that I have had something to concentrate on."

Though Anna's focus and commitment has been questioned, it is obvious that she possesses a great ability to concentrate despite everything that swirls around her.

Interestingly, Anna sees her life as rather mundane compared to how the outside world must view it. "My grandparents, relatives and friends sometimes come see me in America, but it is hard because I rarely stay in one place," she says. "People think this lifestyle is extraordinary, but there is nothing `party' about it. It is just playing and traveling and working."

Between modeling assignments and daily practices, most days leave her exhausted, she says, and in bed by 10. "I have been to nightclubs but they don't excite me much," she told the London *Times*. "They are really not my sort of thing."

Anna likes to read history books and studied via correspondence, at the Physical Culture Academy in Moscow. "People believe because I'm blonde, I must be stupid," she told the Times. "But the blondes are the smart ones. I don't think I have to prove anything to anybody. I just have to go on court and play."

Surely, there will always be those who doubt her, who will see Anna Kournikova as a rich, beautiful tennis player and not much more. And just as surely, she will say they are wrong.

"For me, materialism and money are not the most important thing," Anna says. "The moral part, that's more important than materialism."

> "People believe because I'm blonde, I must be stupid," she told the *Times*. "But the blondes are the smart ones.